NANCY HANKS:
MOTHER OF LINCOLN

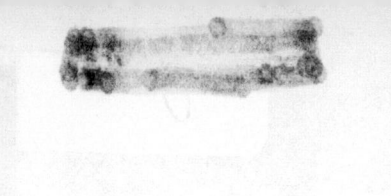

NANCY HANKS: MOTHER OF LINCOLN

by
Charles Ludwig

BAKER BOOK HOUSE
Grand Rapids, Michigan

Library of Congress Catalog Card Number: 65-25475

ISBN: 0-8010-5523-7

**Copyright, 1965, by
Baker Book House Company**

First printing, September 1965
Second printing, October 1967
Third printing, October 1969
Fourth printing, August 1972

Printed in the United States of America

CONTENTS

Prologue		7
1. Tom and Nancy		11
2. Moonlight and Jesse Head		17
3. Tell Me, Betsy		22
4. The Wedding		26
5. Elizabethtown		31
6. Nolin Creek		36
7. A President Is Born		39
8. Knob Creek		46
9. Trouble and Death		53
10. Pigeon Creek		58
11. Church		62
12. The Cabin		66
13. School and Neighbors		71
14. Sorrow		78

Lincoln Homstead State Park is fenced with split rails, just like the ones Kentucky's greatest son used to build. The one-story house, occupying the exact spot where the original stood, is the Lincoln Cabin. Abe's father was reared in the original cabin, built by Abe's grandfather. In the background is the Berry House where Nancy Hanks visited and sewed.
—Courtesy, Travel Division, Frankfort, Kentucky

PROLOGUE

During a prayer meeting at the New York Avenue Presbyterian Church in Washington, D. C., the eyes of two squirming boys wandered idly about the sanctuary, seeking something of interest.

Soon they were drawn to the pastor's study, for silhouetted against the glass door was the familiar profile of President Abraham Lincoln! A little reasoning indicated the shadow was being thrown from a lamp burning near the pastor's desk. This needed investigation, and they could hardly wait until the last *amen* in order to begin.

Enjoying their detective work, they followed the long steps being made in the light snow that had just fallen. The steps led to the White House! When the President arrived at his destination, he threw a tired smile at the youngsters and said, "Thanks for the escort, boys."

The boys, Will Gurley, son of the pastor, and John D. McChesney, soon learned that President Lincoln not only attended the Sunday services with his family, but was also in the habit of attending the prayer services. He usually stayed in the pastor's study with the door slightly ajar so that he could have the inspiration of the services and not become the center of attention.

Abraham Lincoln, contrary to the belief of many, was a man of deep religious convictions. On one occasion he said, "I do not think I could myself be brought to support a man for office whom I knew to be an open enemy of, and scoffer at, religion." His firm belief in a hereafter is shown by the way he dealt with a slave trader who had been sentenced to hang.

His generals frequently criticized him for pardoning deserters and sleeping sentries, but he could be hard with those who bought and sold human beings. He wrote, "Now, therefore, be it known, that I, Abraham Lincoln, President of the United States of America, have granted and do hereby grant unto him, the said Nathaniel Gordon, a respite of the above recited sentence until Friday the twenty-first day of February, a.d. 1862, between the hours of twelve o'clock at noon and three o'clock in the after noon of the said day, when the said sentence shall be executed.

"In granting this respite it becomes my painful duty to admonish the prisoner that, relinquishing all expectation of pardon by Human Authority, he refer himself alone to the mercy of the Common God and Father of all men."

Immediately after the first inauguration, Mary Lincoln secured the seating plan of the New York Avenue Presbyterian Church. Learning that pew number fourteen was vacant, she chose it and she and the family along with the President began to occupy it the next Sunday.

President Lincoln was very fond of his distinguished pastor, Dr. Phineas D. Gurley, and frequently just before a battle would send his carriage for the minister and the two of them would get on their knees at the White House and pray. There were other times when Lincoln preferred to pray alone.

"I went into my room," he said, "and got down on my knees and prayed Almighty God for victory at Gettysburg. I told Him this was His country, the war His war; but that we couldn't stand another Fredricksburg or Chancellorsville. And then and there I made a solemn vow with my Maker that if He would stand by the boys at Gettysburg, I would stand by Him. And He did and I will."

In a sworn affidavit, Mrs. Sidney Lauck, who had joined the New York Avenue Presbyterian Church in 1854, declared, "After Mr. Lincoln's death, Dr. Gurley told me that Mr. Lincoln had made all the necessary arrangements with him and the Session of the New York Avenue Presbyterian Church to be received into the membership of the said church, by confession of his faith in Christ, on the Easter Sunday following the Friday night when Mr. Lincoln was assassinated."*

Abraham Lincoln knew and loved the Bible. In his published papers and recorded conversations he referred to it nearly eighty times, and these quotations came from twenty-two books. Frequently he amazed his friends by locating for them some obscure passage.

Today visitors in the New York Avenue Church can sit in the original Lincoln pew. Although the building is new, the pew is the original one and occupies the same approximate area. Sitting in this pew, one can let his mind follow Lincoln's footsteps back to his beginnings.

The footsteps take one to the Second Inaugural; the immortal Gettysburg Address that will be read as long as men have eyesight; to the signing of the Emancipation Proclamation; and to a host of lesser known things.

Inevitably, however, one must go back through his years of obscurity and hardship to the place of his birth in Hodgenville, Kentucky. There, one can still see the tiny cabin in which he was born.

Hodgenville itself was never very important to Lincoln. He stumbled over the name after his nomination to the Presidency. But Nancy Hanks, the woman who bore him, was extremely important. One day as he was riding along in a buggy with his law partner, William Herndon, the conversation turned to heredity. They were working on a case in the Menard circuit court in which inherited qualities of mind played an important part. Suddenly, his eyes filling with tears, Lincoln exclaimed, "All that I am or ever hope to be I get from my mother. God bless her."

Altogether, President Lincoln had less than one year of formal education. Nevertheless, he was probably our great-

*History of New York Avenue Presbyterian Church, p. 245.

est President, and one of the world's greatest men. There are a number of reasons for this, of course. But the greatest reason was his wonderful mother: Nancy Hanks. The only known records of her writing are on two carefully guarded legal documents where she signed with her mark. One X mark is on the will of Thomas Sparrow, and the other on a deed, transferring the Lincoln Mill Creek farm to Charles Melton.

But her mark of love and faith and morality on young Abe had much more significant results than her marks with a pen. That mark helped bring freedom to every slave in the United States. Because of this, her life is extremely important to us.

1. TOM AND NANCY

A little startled by the low nickering of a horse, Nancy Hanks cautiously peered through the open cabin window where she was living. Then her heart began to race, for standing by the silvery trunk of the front yard's largest beech tree was one of the most popular men of the community—young Tom Lincoln.

Nancy watched him as one transfixed. Her blue-green eyes followed each move. Slowly, methodically, he tethered his horse to one of the spreading limbs. Then, with a manner of one who knows what he's doing, he headed for the cabin.

Tethering his horse to a solid limb meant that he intended to stay for a while, and the fashionable jeans he was carelessly wearing meant that he wanted to make a good impression. But why would he want to impress her? The last she remembered, he was paying close attention to Sarah, the attractive daughter of Christopher Bush.

But there was no time to think about this now. Tom was already striding up the path between the rows of yellow daffodils that stretched from the cabin to the yard. In a moment he would be at the door. Quickly she slipped into her shoes, pulled a wide horn comb through her long, dark hair with smooth, practiced strokes. Then she wound it above her high forehead and pinned it in place with a comb. She would have used hairpins, but she didn't have any; nor did any of the other girls in the community. Hairpins had not yet penetrated backwoods Kentucky.

Tom sat awkwardly in the splint-bottomed chair to which Nancy had nervously pointed him. "I—I've been thinkin' about you fur a long time," he began, speaking in a slow drawl. "Every time I see you at a meetin' in a cabin or at the meetin' house I think about you. I can't seem to get you out of my mind." As he spoke, a self-conscious smile lit up his grey eyes and round face. "I-I-I've been wonderin' if I could come and see you once in a while. That is if Tom and Betsy Sparrow don't mind." He finished lamely, his eyes searching the floor.

Nancy felt warm color creeping up her neck. Tom Lincoln was a clean man. He didn't swear or get drunk. He loved the Bible and with some effort could sign his name, something very few of his neighbors could do. Moreover, he was already a landlord even though he was only in his late twenties. Gossip said that he had paid Dr. John Toms Slater 118 pounds for the Mill Creek farm. That was a pile of money, and he had paid it in cash. He now had tenants on the farm and was picking up a few extra dollars from his carpenter work in Elizabethtown.

"Uncle Tom and Aunt Betsy won't mind," she said, flushing an even deeper crimson, for sometimes she called her uncle and aunt Ma and Pa, especially if the company didn't know the difference. "You can come whenever you like and you'll be right welcome. Only I'm not always here. My sewing takes me into other people's homes. Sometimes when I'm sewing for a wedding I'm gone as much as two weeks."

"I've heard that you can read," said Tom, swallowing hard as he sought a means of conversation. He nodded toward the Bible above the fireplace. "Get it down and show me," he added, running strong fingers through his coarse, black hair.

"Yes, my real mother, Lucy Sparrow, taught me," said Nancy, getting up and going after the thickly-bound volume. "She can both read and write! There aren't many round here that can do that." In her excitement she nearly knocked over the big spinning wheel standing in the corner.

"What should I read?" she asked, going back to her chair.

"Just read anything," said Tom. "I just want to see if

you can. I know some preachers—good ones, too—that can't read. They have to get someone else to read fur 'em."

Nancy opened the book and haltingly read the Twenty-third Psalm.

"You do very well, Nancy," exclaimed Tom, "and I'm mighty proud of you. I'll be braggin' about your readin' wherever I go."

Suddenly the leather-hinged door flew open and young Dennis Hanks bounded into the cabin. He cast a long look at Tom and then fled to Nancy for refuge, grabbing her loose-fitting linsey-woolsey dress in his grubby fists.

"Don't mind him," laughed Nancy. "He's my Aunt Nancy's boy, and he's only six. There are just too many Nancy's in our family! That's why they call her Big Nancy and me Little Nancy."

"My youngest sister is another Nancy," said Tom, "and there are several other Nancys in Hardin County, and at least one of them is Nancy Hanks."

"Just don't get us mixed up!" said Nancy, her blue-green eyes brightening.

Soon the door opened and Tom and Betsy Sparrow stepped in. "Well, I guess I must be on my way," said Tom Lincoln after he had been introduced. At the door he turned to Nancy, and for a brief moment their eyes met. Then Tom said, "Nancy, Jesse Head is goin' to be at Elizabethtown real soon. He's one of the best preachers that ever preached in Kentucky. How about me and you goin' over to hear him?"

"I'll go if I can," replied Nancy eagerly. "I'd sure like to hear him."

"And when I come back, Dennis," grinned Tom over his shoulder, "I'll tell you how my pappy, Abraham, was killed by Indians, and how they almost killed me when I was just your age."

"What do you think of him, Aunt Betsy?" asked Nancy, after the clip-clop of his horse's hoofs had faded away.

"I—I really don't know, Nancy," replied Betsy thoughtfully. "For a while I was sure he was going to marry Sarah Bush, but I guess Daniel Johnston, the jailer in Elizabethtown, got her away from him. Tom Lincoln does have a terrible temper. A while back he bit the end of a man's nose off—bit it off slick as a whistle."

"Oh, how horrible!" gasped Nancy, a sick feeling filling her stomach.

"But tell her the rest of the story, Betsy," chided her husband, raising his voice. "He bit it off because the fellow had insulted a woman! Tom's a mighty fine man. And he's been converted recently. If he wants to marry you, you'd better say yes. That's what I think in a nutshell."

"He also spends a lot of time telling stories," said Betsy, sharply on the defensive.

"Yes, but his stories are clean," retorted Tom Sparrow with warmth, "and there's nothing wrong with a clean story—especially if it's so funny it would make a calf laugh. And that's the kind Tom Lincoln tells. The other day, over at Hodgen's Mill, while I was waiting to get my flour, I heard him tell a story I'll never forget.

"It seems that a widower remarried, and one day his second wife said to him, 'Thomas, we have lived together a long time and you have not yet told me whom you like best, your first wife or me.' Thomas replied, 'Oh, now, Sarah, that reminds me of old John Hardin . . . who had a fine looking pair of horses, and a neighbor coming in one day and looking at them said, 'John, which horse do you like best?' John said, 'I can't tell; one of them kicks and the other bites and I don't know which is wust.'"

That evening as Nancy watched the last splinters of the sun glow on the stark ribs of Mildraugh's Hill, she got out a mirror and studied herself. She did not have the fine dark curls of Sarah Bush, but there was nothing in her angular face for which she should be ashamed. She noticed her high forehead, firm, pointed chin; her dark, luxuriant hair and slightly dark skin.

The scales, she remembered, said that she weighed one hundred and thirty-five pounds. But this wasn't too much, for the mark on the cabin door indicated that she was five feet eight inches tall. This was one inch shorter than Tom Lincoln!

"What you doin'?" asked Tom Sparrow, slipping up on her unexpectedly. "Are you wonderin' if you're beautiful enough fur that carpenter Tom Lincoln? Well you are, and no mistake about it. You're as pretty a gal as I've ever seen. You ain't got nothin' to worry about. Not a thing."

Shocked by all of this flattery, Nancy faced him speechless.

"By the way," he continued, "Richard Berry wants you to go over to his house at the end of the week. His old lady has a lot of sewin' to be done, and since you're the best seamstress in Kentucky he wants you."

As Nancy knelt by her bed, she remembered that a short while before she had prayed in a cabin filled with people, "Jesus, I give everything to thee. I give thee all. I give thee all. I am wholly thine!" Now she repeated the prayer, and asked for special guidance during the months to come. Then she blew out the candle and slipped under the bearskin her uncle had given her.

She tried to sleep, but the events of the evening kept parading before her; and when she did get to sleep, she dreamed of men with various sized noses, and of one man with a nose that had been bitten off. The last part of the dream awakened her, and so she knelt in prayer again. Then she returned to bed and went sound asleep.

At the breakfast table Dennis took an enormous bite of cornbread, and then, speaking around it, said, "I shore hope that man comes back and tells me about them Injuns."

"You shouldn't speak with your mouth so full, Dennis," scolded Betsy Sparrow. "It just ain't good manners."

"But I do hope he comes," said Dennis, speaking around another bite even larger than the first.

2. MOONLIGHT AND JESSE HEAD

There were no windows in the modest log church at Elizabethtown where Jesse Head had been announced to preach, and so when Tom and Nancy took their seats, the front of the building was shrouded in darkness even though the sun was still high in the sky. The light that did reach into the building came from the open door where people were standing around in denims and buckskin. There was just enough of it for Nancy to notice the speaker's long nose and slightly curled roof of red hair.

"Our speaker this evenin' needs no introduction," said William Downs, a visiting minister. "He's probably married more couples in Washington County than any preacher in Kentucky. He is a man of many skills. He is a justice of the peace, the President of the Board of Trustees in Springfield, a deacon in the Methodist Church and a very able preacher. He's in demand everywhere. We're just plumb fortunate to be able to get him."

Jesse Head preached to the crowded congregation with great enthusiasm. He clapped his hands and stomped his foot to emphasize a point. He thumped the Bible and pointed his long index finger. But his sermon lasted only an hour, about half the length of other men's sermons. In it, he denounced sin of every description, warned of hell and judgment and pointed men and women to heaven by the way of the Cross. He declared that there was no salvation except through the new birth. The congregation sang many hymns including "Rock of Ages," and another, a part of which went:

"You may bury me in the east,
You may bury me in the west,
And we'll all ri-ise together in the morning."

The rhythm of this was so definite, and the meaning so clear, Nancy felt an ecstasy flow through her body.

As they walked out after the benediction Tom said, "When I get married Brother Head is goin' to tie the knot. That way it will be a strong knot, fur he'll tie it as a preacher and also as a justice of the peace!"

"But you're a Baptist and he's a Methodist," said Nancy, laughing at his reasoning.

"That don't make no difference to me. I figger we're all goin' to the same place anyhow. When my sister, Nancy, married William Brumfield, Thomas Kyle done the hitchin' and he's a Campbellite. Only trouble with the Methodists is they're afraid to get their feet wet! Jesse Head's my man."*

> "There is a man in our town,
> Who walks the street in a dressing-gown;
> His nose is long and his hair is red,
> And he goes by the name of Jesse Head."

As Tom and Nancy stood around visiting with the people, William Downs joined them. "Nancy, this is Brother Downs," said Tom. "He's a right smart preacher. Says he's goin' to start a Baptist church in our community one of these days. He's one man that's really plumb against slavery, and that suits me just fine."

From the meetin' house, which also served as a school, Tom and Nancy rode through the main part of Elizabethtown. The city was growing and Tom was proud of it. "When I get married E-town's where I want to live," he said. Most of the houses were made of logs; some of hewn logs; and there was one three-story house made of brick,

---

*In 1830 Jesse Head began to publish *The American*, a Democratic paper in Harrodsburg, Kentucky. This paper was opposed by a rival, called *The Union*. This sheet ridiculed Head with some pointed doggerel:

and another two-story one with marble steps. There was a tannery, a brick yard, four blacksmiths, a tailor, a shoemaker, a distillery and three stores. One of the stores was run by John J. Audubon, who was always watching and studying birds. As the city grew, the people became more fashionable. Most of the men wore coon-skin hats, but here and there a gay blade sported a beaver. One of the lawyers—and there was an overabundance of lawyers*—was a real dandy. He swaggered about in a powdered wig, knee-breeches, stockings, low shoes and silver buckles on his knees. Another lawyer was dressed just as well, but in addition he had a slave follow him at just the proper distance while he rode in pomp on a fancy horse.

"Now I want to show you some timbers I'm hewing for Denton Geoghegan," said Tom. "He's goin' to use 'em to build a mill. He has plenty of money and should do well."

They visited his place of work, viewed the timbers and then Nancy said, "You know, Tom, we'd better get back home. It's quite a way and Dennis just can't wait until you tell him about that Indian who killed your father. He's been pesterin' me night and day."

"Well, you see," said Tom, facing the Sparrows and Nancy and Dennis from a place by the fire, "my father, Abraham, owned a big farm on Linville Creek in Augusta County, Virginia. It was there I was born on January 6, 1778. Pa's farm was a good one. He made money on it, but he was a restless man. During the Revolution they piled the taxes on until Pa couldn't stand it. Then one day Daniel Boone—a distant relative of his—came to see us. Boone told him that we should move to Kentucky. He said the rivers were wide and full of fish; that there were great valleys full of fertile land; that there were tall mountains, great forests and lots

---

*There were so many lawyers a law was passed limiting two lawyers to each side in a lawsuit.

of game. He also said the land could be had at forty cents an acre. This was enough for Pa.

"In 1780 he made a trip over here. The trip showed him ol' Boone had been speakin' the truth. And so he sold his Virginia land for a big price and we moved to Kentucky where he bought thousands of acres. I wasn't more 'n an infant in them days. But I've heard the story so often it seems I kin remember it. We had to follow the Wilderness Road, through the Cumberland Gap over old buffalo trails. Sometimes we had to wade rivers, and sometimes we nearly drowned in the rain. And always we had to keep lookin' fur Indians. They had a way of keepin' their tomahawks and scalpin' knives handy.

"Pa had two thousand acres on Green River, and good land in other places. He just went plumb wild over Kentucky. 'Bathsheba,' he says to Ma, 'this is the greatest land on earth.' One day just after he had put in a crop, me and my brothers, Josiah and Mordecai, were out with him when suddenly we heard a shot. The next moment Pa crumpled up in front of us. Mordecai and Josiah took to their heels. But I couldn't run as fast as they, because I was only about the age of Dennis here, and besides I didn't want to leave Pa. I thought he might still have some life in him. But he was plumb dead. As he lay all quiet in front of me I can tell you I had an awful feelin'. He'd been talkin' one minute and the next minute he was dead.

"While I was watchin' him, my brothers ran into a nearby fort. Mordecai kept his eye on me through a crack between the logs. Suddenly he saw an Indian all covered with war paint come out into the clearing and head fur me. He didn't know for sure what the Indian was goin' to do, and so he slipped the long barrel of his rifle through the crack and waited. Soon the Indian bent down and took me by the hand.

"Just then Mordecai got a bead on an ornament around

his neck and pulled the trigger. Mordecai was a good shot and the Indian fell over dead almost on top of me."*

"You were saved through a miracle," said Nancy. "But I'm sorry your father had to die. He must have been a good man. And I'm also sorry the Indian died. Shootin' people never does any good. Never!"

But the story was interesting and Tom's slow drawl made it come to life and filled it with suspense. Nancy had a deep pride in her heart for Tom, even though she knew she'd have to repeat the story every day for Dennis.

A full moon was high over Muldraugh's Hill when Tom Lincoln finally stepped through the cabin door. Nancy followed him to his horse, tethered to the beech tree. They lingered there for a long time, standing together in a splash of bright moonlight. Then Tom mounted his horse and rode away.

Nancy's heart beat wildly as she watched him disappear around a bend, over a knoll and into the shadows. A hundred sounds of the wild filled the air—the chirp of crickets, deep-throated croaks of the frogs; the sway of the trees; the splash of water; the hoot of an owl and the distant call of a wolf.

It seemed to her that all of the sounds were in harmony, and that they were playing a magnificent song—a song of love—just for her.

She paused again at the cabin door. A faraway look filled her eyes. Then with a prayer of joy in her heart she closed the door.

"That was a good story," said Dennis from his bearskin by the fireplace.

"Yes, it was," replied Nancy. "It was a very good story."

---

*Some scholars think Abraham may have been killed on some land that is now covered by the city of Louisville.

3. TELL ME, BETSY

The spring drifted into a humid summer. And then came a magnificent fall that found Nancy and Tom walking together along the red paths that twisted down to the springs, over the hills, and through the valleys. These paths, known so well by the pioneers, were soft with oak and maple and beech leaves that had fallen from the trees that were now beginning to stand naked and defiant throughout the land. The leaves had turned, or were turning, a dozen dramatic colors or more. Some had changed to scarlet; others to a deep or light brown; others to many shades of burnished yellow; and still others, stubborn to the end, remained a steady green with only their curled edges changing color.

The conversations of Tom and Nancy tended to become longer and quieter and more to the point and further from the point. They held hands and their grips became tighter, and the faraway look in their eyes became deeper.

One evening as the slender fingers of the sun were beginning to clench in a tight red fist, Tom moved closer to Nancy on the bank of the river, and summed up all his feelings in four short words, "I love you, Nancy," he drawled, brushing her hair with his lips.

"I love you, too, Tom," she replied.

The winter that year was beautiful. The trees filled with snow and the snow on the slopes of Muldraugh's Hill gleamed white in the sun. The rabbits and the deer left tracks in the snow, and Tom Lincoln became a regular visitor at the home of Thomas and Betsy Sparrow.

But about the time the rivers began to freeze over, Nancy felt a chill in her heart. Her food lost its taste and she began almost to dread the sound of Tom's knock on the door.

"What's the matter, Nancy?" asked Betsy.

"Oh, nothing," she replied, making an effort to stop the tears squeezing from her eyes.

"She's just lovesick," scoffed Thomas Sparrow.

"If you would tell me what's wrong, I might be able to help you," said Betsy, trying to understand.

Instead of answering, Nancy grabbed a bucket and headed for the spring. The ache in her heart was so great she felt that she could not stand it, and pray as she would, it would not leave. The tears came in a sudden flood and dripped on the ice as she chipped it away in order to fill her bucket. She prayed again for wisdom, and then headed back slowly toward the cabin while a cold wind rumpled her hair and brought a dark blush to her cheeks.

Nancy was working on some linsey-woolsey at her loom when she felt the time had come when she should share her problem with Aunt Betsy.

"Mother," she said, "I think you know that I love Tom more than life itself, but all this winter I've been thinking that I'm not really worthy of him...."

"Don't say that, Nancy," replied Betsy, moving her chair over to the loom. "You're a smart girl. You can even read, and you're a Christian. Besides, you've lived a good life."

"It isn't that," said Nancy, pausing with a shuttle of wool thread in her right hand. She paused for a long moment, as she sought to control her tears. "What worries me is that you're not my real mother, and I've never known who my father is. I-I don't think it's fair for Tom to marry me and not know the truth. I...."

"Well, Nancy, I do know a lot of the truth in the matter and I think you should know it, and I'm going to tell you," said Betsy kindly. "While we were living in Virginia, your mother, that is my sister Lucy Hanks, fell for a man; and like a lot of other girls, she lost her head and made a mistake. You were born in a log cabin on the slopes of Mike's Run* on February 5, 1784. I remember the time very well. You were an unusually long baby, and everyone said you were very bright just like your mother who was smarter than any of the rest of us.

"Your grandfather, Joseph Hanks, who was my father, tried to get Lucy to tell him who your father was. But she always refused. This, I think, is why he cut her out of his will.** After he died in 1793 all of the children but Lucy were given a cow or a horse.

"Right after you were born Pa mortgaged his farm in Virginia to Peter Putnam, one of our neighbors, for twenty-one pounds and nine shillings. This wasn't very much, but Pa was anxious to get some money so that we could move to Kentucky. He never intended to pay back the money, and so when it came due he lost the farm. That was one of the best bargains Putnam ever had.

"We all moved to Kentucky in 1784, just after you were born. Lucy had quite a time with you on the trip. Sometimes you'd start yellin' and nothing on earth would stop you. And so that's the story Nancy. It's not a pretty story, but it's the truth."

"I knew most of this, Aunt Betsy; and I know I must accept the truth. But for a long time I've heard people whispering that Mother got into trouble after the family moved to Kentucky.... Tell me about that."

"Lucy was accused of being wayward by the Grand Jury, but it never came to court. Just about that time, Henry Sparrow, my husband's brother, fell in love with her. And, in spite of all the gossip, he believed she was

*Nancy's birthplace has now been reconstructed. It is on a tributary of Patterson Creek in Mineral County, West Virginia—a short distance from Cumberland, Maryland. This was in Virginia before the Civil War.
**The will has been preserved at Bardstown, Kentucky.

24

a good woman. And, maybe to prove this, Henry and Lucy bought their marriage license in 1790 and didn't get married until almost a year later.*

"During this time, Lucy lived such a good life all the gossip stopped. Your foster father, Henry, is a good man, a wonderful man. He fought with George Washington and was at the surrender of Cornwallis at Yorktown.

"You ought also to know that George Washington himself surveyed one side of our farm in Virginia. That isn't much, but it's something to talk about on cold nights . . . . "

Nancy deftly threw the wool shuttle between the linen threads—the warp—on her loom and pushed it into place with the long, smooth batten. "I'm glad to know that Mother lived down her reputation, and proved to everyone that she's a good woman," said Nancy, some of the tenseness out of her voice.

"Of course she's a good woman, Nancy. You have every right to be proud of her. Remember she taught you to read! Besides, it isn't what the other person does that matters. It's what we do ourselves that really counts. There is no reason at all, Nancy, why you shouldn't hold your head high. You're a good girl and I'm mighty proud of you!"

---

*Lucy Hank's marriage application in her own handwriting is on file. It covers a piece of paper about four by five inches and reads:
"I do sertify that I am of age and give my
approbation freely for henry Sparrow to git our Lisons
this or enny other day.
given under my hand this day.
Apriel 26th, 1790
Lucey Hanks

Test:
Robert Michel
John bery.

4. THE WEDDING

Since weddings in backwoods Kentucky were nearly as scarce as school teachers in 1806, the frontier guests who crowded the Richard Berry log cabin on Thursday, June 12, for Tom and Nancy's wedding were reasonably excited. The Washington County Court, which was in session, even dismissed for the day. This, however, was not because of the importance of either the bride or the groom. Rather, it was because the minister, the best man—perhaps Mordecai Lincoln—and Richard Berry, who gave the bride away, were all involved in its proceedings.

Although there are many uncertainties about this wedding, we can all be certain that not a single guest realized that it was destined to be one of history's most important occasions. After all, Tom and Nancy were merely neighbors. Both were orphans. Both were nearly illiterate. And both were from undistinguished families. Indeed, it may be that many of the guests were secretly more interested in the feast that was to follow than in the ceremony!

Tom Lincoln made careful preparations for the wedding. Because of court records and account books kept by local merchants, we learn that he bought a beaver hat for one pound and six shillings; a pair of suspenders for a dollar and a half; "five yards of linen," "four skeins of silk," "one yard of calico cloth," "three and a half yards of cassemere," and one and a half yards of "red flannel."

On June 10, he and his friend Richard Berry rode over to Springfield, the county-seat, and secured his marriage bond, the legal document that was frequently used as a marriage license in those days. Fortunately, this bond has been preserved. It can be seen at the Washington County Courthouse in Springfield, Kentucky. It reads: "Know all men by these presents that we, Thomas Lincoln and Richard Berry, are held and firmly bound unto his Excellency the Governor of Kentucky, for the interest and full sum of fifty pounds money to the payment of which well and truly to be made to the said Governor and his successors, we bind ourselves, our heirs etc. and we jointly and severally promise by these presents sealed with our seals and dated this 10th day of June, 1806. The condition of the above bond, obligation, is such that whereas there is a marriage shortly intended between the above bounded Thomas Lincoln and Nancy Hanks, for which arrangements have been made; now if there be no lawful cause to obstruct this marriage, then this obligation to be null and void or else to be and remain in full force and virtue by law."

When Tom signed it, he was twenty-eight years of age.

The Berry cabin at Beech Fork of Salt River near Beechland was selected for the ceremony for a number of reasons. Probably the most important one was that it was in Washington County where many of Tom's relatives lived. Another is because of the deep friendship between Nancy and the Berrys.

The one-room cabin stood on a grassy knoll in a thick clump of trees. If the Berrys were like their neighbors there were two rows of daffodils running from their front door to the yard. At this time of the year the delicate blooms were gone. But there was plenty of color, for the roses were in full blossom. As the people gathered they tethered their horses to the limber beech branches and parked their ox-wagons in the cool shade.

Some of the men wore buckskin breeches and hunting shirts. The more fashionable ones were clad in freshly scrubbed jeans. The women came dressed in homespun, made of thread produced on their own spinning wheels. While earlier guests waited for the knot to be tied, they visited, swapped yarns, courted, and perhaps even traded horses.

Jesse Head, just turned thirty-eight, rode up on a gray mare late in the afternoon. A little early, he moved his

This building houses the Berry Cabin where Nancy Hanks and Tom Lincoln were married by Jesse Head on June 12, 1806.
—Courtesy, Department of Public Information, Frankfort, Kentucky

saddle to the back of the mount so that his horse would not scald in the hot, humid weather. Then he went around among the guests, shaking their hands, asking about the news and encouraging them to attend church services.

While the fat Negro cook—the Berrys had a number of slaves—prepared the food another slave tuned his fiddle and began to play the popular tunes of the time: "Turkey in the Straw"; "The Girl I Left Behind Me"; "Sugar in the Gourd"; and "The Money Musk."

A person who was present remembered: "We had bear meat, venison, wild turkey and ducks, eggs, wild and tame, maple sugar lumps tied on a string to bite off for coffee . . . syrup in big gourds, peach and honey, a sheep barbecued whole over coals of wood burned in a pit, and covered with green boughs to keep the juices in."

What was Nancy's outfit like? No one really knows; but from what Tom bought, it would seem that it contained linen and silk and at least some of the red cloth and "cassemere." And we can be sure that it was beautifully made, for Nancy had lavished her best skill on it. One of her helpers, no doubt, was Betsy Sparrow. These two, working in harmony with love and care, must have produced an eye-catching trousseau.

We do not have a roster of the guests. But certainly among them was Tom's mother, Bathsheba; Thomas and Betsy Sparrow; Mr. and Mrs. Henry Sparrow; Tom's brothers along with their families; young Dennis, and a host of others.

When the sun neared the horizon, Nancy and Tom stood before Deacon Head. Perhaps they faced the fireplace. The usual questions were asked. The usual replies were given. And then, the red-haired preacher pronounced them "joined together in the Holy Estate of Matrimony agreeable to the rules of the Methodist Episcopal Church."

The feast was served by slaves, moving in and out of the candle-lit cabin with heaping trays in their hands. Tom and Nancy joined in the feast, graciously received the best wishes of their friends, and then, while the guests lingered over their food, they excused themselves and headed for Elizabethtown where they had arranged to start housekeeping.

5. ELIZABETHTOWN

William Herndon visited the house in Elizabethtown where the Lincolns had lived and described it as accurately as he could. "It is a very sorry building and nearly bare of furniture. It is about fourteen feet square, has been three times removed, twice used as a slaughter house and once as a stable."

Tom and Nancy, however, didn't mind it at all; for it was not a great deal worse than the cabins of their neighbors. Besides, they were more interested in each other than in the house. But they did have at least a few things a new bride would need. We know this, for we have a record of some of the things they bought at the Bleakley and Montgomery store two days after the wedding. The store's musty accounts show that they purchased "½ set knives & forks" and "three skanes silk." Later, Tom went to the "Thomas McIntire Sale" and bid in "a dish and plate for $2.68" and "a basin and spoons" at $3.24.

Nancy, living away from her real mother most of her life, had become an excellent cook. Her corn bread, "hog and hominy," and vegetables were as well prepared as any in E-town. She stirred the meal in a wide wooden bowl with water and a pinch of salt. Next she scooped the thick dough in her hand, tossed it gracefully back and forth between her cupped palms until it was the right shape, and then cast it neatly into the oven. From five to six "pones" were baked at a time and they were good eating. Nancy took pride in her cooking, and although she was not equal to the woman who legend said could toss a pancake up the chimney, rush outside, and catch it in her pan, she could prepare a tasty meal.

Tom liked the food she prepared, and when he returned from work he let her know it, with both words of appreciation and action. But Tom never ate anything without first saying grace. His usual prayer was: "Fit and prepare us for humble service, we beg for Christ's sake. Amen."

Nancy joined Tom in prayers, and frequently read out loud to him from the Ostervald Bible.* The Severens Valley Baptist Church in Elizabethtown was the oldest church of its denomination in Kentucky. And, although there is no indication that Tom and Nancy ever joined, we can almost be certain that they attended. Reverend Josiah Dodge was the pastor. He also preached at the Nolin Church, and although it was an extremely delicate subject, he took his stand against slavery.

Tom learned to supplement his income by making coffins. When death occurred in a family, a member would measure the corpse with a long stick and take it to Tom. Tom made his coffins an inch longer at the top than at the bottom and fastened the boards together with wooden pegs that he whittled out with a jackknife. A child's coffin brought three dollars, a woman's six and a man's seven.

E-town was full of colorful stories about the past and the Lincolns heard most of them. Tom delighted in stories and often repeated them with an added relish to his friends.

The town's first jail set the treasury back $42.60. This

---

*Notations on this Bible show that it was once sold for $5.00 and that the original price was "27 shillings." This later price was then altered to read: "30 shillings." President Lincoln took it to the White House and kept it on his desk. Large sections have been carefully torn out. The following parts are missing: all of Matthew through Mark VIII, 6; Exodus IX to XVIII; II Maccabees XII. It is thought these pages were removed and sold in order to acquire more Lincoln relics. President Lincoln's fondness for Isaiah is shown by the way Isaiah XLV, XLVI and XLVIII are thumbed and worn.

The fourteen foot by fourteen foot house in Elizabethtown, Kentucky, where Tom and Nancy started housekeeping. It stood near the courthouse.
—Courtesy, National Archives

jail never satisfied the sheriff. He claimed it was inadequate and was not a worthy building for the city. As a result of his agitation a new jail was built at the staggering cost of $700. This new building was complete with stocks and an up-to-date whipping post. Drunks were laid on their backs with their feet secured in the stocks until they were sober. Others were forced to kneel with their heads and arms fastened between the smooth, grooved planks.

Many were imprisoned for debt. One man, imprisoned because he couldn't pay his bills, set the jail on fire and narrowly escaped being burned to death. He was then convicted of arson; but when it was discovered that he could lay brick he was pardoned. There was a shortage of bricklayers in E-town!

There were many barefoot children on the streets, for it was quite common for a family to have a dozen or more offspring. But food was cheap. Eggs could be had for five cents a dozen.

Tom's affairs were coasting along very well when suddenly Denton Geoheagan informed him that he was not going to pay for the timber he had cut for his proposed mill. This was a blow, for Tom and Nancy had been counting on this money. In desperation, Tom sued and won. Then Geoheagan sued Tom, claiming the timbers were not hewn properly. Tom won the suit, and then Geoheagan sued again. Again Tom won, and the bill was settled out of court.

Tom got his money, but there were many anxious moments for him and Nancy. This anxiety sent them to their knees in prayer.

Soon after they were married, Nancy learned that she was going to have a baby. Filled with joy over the news, she worked steadily at her spinning wheel and loom making cloth that could be sewn into dressers or shirts for the new one. Thoughts of the new baby and the rhythm of the spinning wheel and loom filled her with a new ecstasy. Sometimes as she worked she sang:

> "Lo! here 'twixt Heaven and Earth I swing,
> And whilst the shuttle swiftly flies,
> With cheerful heart I work and sing
> And envy none beneath the skies."

At other times she hummed or sang her favorite hymn, a hymn she had learned from her mother and one that was a favorite throughout Kentucky:

> "Come, Thou fount of every blessing
> Tune my heart to sing Thy praise."

Nancy's first baby was born on February 10, 1807. She was a stubby little girl with dark grey eyes and dark brown hair. Some said she looked just like Nancy; others contended she looked like Tom; and still others declared she looked like both of them. Nancy had a friend who had named her first daughter *Nancy*; and so Nancy Lincoln returned the compliment by naming her baby *Sarah*.

Inspired by his growing family, Tom worked even harder at his carpentry. The little family would need security and he was determined they would have it. He bought two new lots in Elizabethtown. He became a respected citizen and the people believed in him.

He was summoned to jury duty and given a job guarding prisoners. On December 12, 1808, Tom bought a 348½-acre farm from Isaac Bush. He paid $200 for it and assumed a small obligation to a former title holder. This farm was on the South Fork of Nolin Creek, eighteen miles southeast of E-town. There was a wonderful spring that could be reached by going down several steps into a cave. The water never came to the surface. It flowed away in a subterranean channel, but it was clear, pure, adequate, and added great value to the farm.

Nancy was overjoyed to know they owned this land, for their cabin on it would be only two miles from the Thomas Sparrows, and she longed to live closer to Betsy. There was no store or village nearby. But they would live close to Hodgen's Mill where she could get her corn ground.

There was also a Baptist church in the area where Brother Josiah Dodge preached once a month.

6. NOLIN CREEK

Nolin Creek, like so many areas in Kentucky, received its name from a story. A preacher named Lynn, who lived near Hodgen's Mill, went on a long hike and never returned. A searching party was sent after him only to discover that he had been killed by Indians. On its return, the leader shook his head, shrugged his shoulders and announced, "No Lynn."

Although the Nolin farm was not as fertile as the Mill Creek farm, Tom and Nancy were eager to move there. But for some reason that scholars have never been able to discover, they were not able to move onto it right away. Instead, they moved to a very crude house in a grove of wild crab-apples trees on a farm owned by George Brownfield. Here, near the village of Buffalo, Tom worked for Mr. Brownfield and did other odd jobs.

The crab apples in the grove grew in great abundance, and the people came from long distances to gather them. That summer while the wild fragrance of the blossoms filled the air, and wide-winged hawks circled above, Nancy learned that she was to become a mother again. This was good news for Tom and gave him added incentive to get a cabin ready on Nolin Creek. Secretly, he hoped Nancy would have a son—a son that might be named Abraham after his father.

The question of slavery was making a great stir in Kentucky at this time. In 1800 Lexington, Kentucky, had a population of 1,797. Of the inhabitants of this most progressive city, 439 were slaves. Nashville, Tennessee, listed 355 inhabitants and 141 of these—nearly half—were slaves. In Washington County there was nearly one slave for every white man over twenty-one.

Slavery was an open sore.

There were ministers who owned slaves and who quoted Scripture trying to prove that it was quite moral for them to own slaves. Other ministers publicly stood out against slavery and pounded the dust out of their Bibles proving their point. The agitation became so bitter that churches and entire denominations were split over the problem.

Two of the great denominations in Kentucky asked their ministers to stop agitating against slavery; and one of them, in 1808, ceased to forbid their members from owning slaves. There was no point in "disturbing the peace in Zion," especially over such a small conscience question!

The Baptists, however, kept up the agitation and formed the first anti-slavery organization in the state—The Kentucky Abolition Society. Most of its members came from the "Baptized Licking-Locust Association, Friends of Humanity." It was a dynamic, two-fisted organization.

On the third Saturday of July, 1808, the South Fork Church—not far from Tom Lincoln's new farm—had a split over this issue. The records say there was a "rent off from the church on account of slavery." The fifteen members who left probably joined the Little Mount Church, some three miles from Hodgen's Mill, in the general direction of Muldraugh's Hill. This was a Primitive Baptist Church that took a definite stand against slavery in all its forms. William Downs, an old friend of the Lincolns, was its pastor.

William E. Barton and others think that Tom and Nancy made this congregation their church home, and they have excellent reasons for this conclusion. It is very probable, however, that the Lincolns also attended services in many other places. They loved to hear the Word preached. Revivals and camp-meetings in those days were very popular and were charged with fervent emotion.

Peter Cartwright, who lived to become a political rival

of Abe Lincoln, published his famous autobiography in 1856. In this colorful book he describes a backwoods camp-meeting that he conducted: "The meeting was protracted for weeks, and was kept up day and night. Thousands heard of the mighty work and came on foot, on horseback and in wagons. It was supposed there were in attendance at different times from twelve to twenty-five thousand. Hundreds fell prostrate under the mighty power of God as men slain in battle; and it was supposed that between one and two thousand souls were happily and powerfully converted to God during the meetings. It was not unusual for as many as seven preachers to be addressing the listening thousands at the same time from different stands. At times, more than a thousand persons broke into loud shoutings all at once, and the shouts could be heard for miles around."

As the bees sought the crab-apple blossoms, Nancy kept busy with her spinning wheel and loom. Each day she longed to hear Tom say that they would move by the end of the week. She always felt more secure when she lived on her own land.

Finally, the great day came. Nancy loaded her things into the wagon and with little Sarah in her arms she and Tom bounced over the wilderness road to their new home.

7. A PRESIDENT IS BORN

The cabin on the South Fork of Nolin Creek was fresh and much larger than the shack in Elizabethtown. It was almost eighteen by sixteen feet. And, although the floor was of dirt, it had been packed down and swept clean. The carefully-chinked walls were made of hewn logs and had been skilfully fitted together at the ends. The cabin was snug and weather-tight.

Nancy's bed was made of selected poles, held in place with long cleats attached to the wall and supported on one leg. The large chimney standing on the ground behind the adequate stone fireplace was made of small logs and sticks cemented together with big chunks of clay so that it would draw.

Tom had arranged for a big pile of wood to be ready by the fireplace when Nancy moved in. This was an extra surprise.

A quick glance confirmed where each item should be, for Nancy had been thinking about it a long time. The pots and pans and shovel and tongs were placed on the opposite side of the wood by the fireplace. Then a soft bearskin was rolled out in front. Next, she arranged the table and chairs in the center and moved the loom and spinning wheel near the back wall.

"You shore know how to make it look nice," said Tom, after he had slipped his long-barrelled rifle onto the pegs above the leather-hinged door.

Without answering, Nancy stood at a far corner and viewed her work with a critical eye. She was silent for a long moment and nervously tapped her teeth while she considered. "Tom, there's one more thing we need," she said, stepping forward. "Go out to the wagon and bring in them two bunches of corn—the bright red and yellow ones with the braided husks.

"Now hold them here," she said, pointing to a place above the spinning wheel, "while I have a look." She stepped over to the firewood and studied the scene. "Now move 'em a little toward the door. That's right. Now separate them a little and nail 'em down. And when you get through with that, go over to Aunt Betsy's and bring a long-necked gourd and that little bearskin she borrowed a while back. I want to hang them by the door."

When each treasured possession was in place, Tom and Nancy stood by the fire and admired their little home. "It's wonderful, Nancy," said Tom, pressing his cheek to hers. "You ought to be one of them artists like John J. Audubon over at E-town. Only if you do, don't spend all your time paintin' birds!"

Nancy was thankful for her new home and enjoyed showing it off to visitors. She was especially thankful for the nearby spring, the one that is now called Sinking Spring. It saved her many steps, and with Sarah to look after and the new one coming, she needed all the energy she could manage.

At home, alone, she liked to sit by the fireplace. Sometimes she read from the Bible or a stray newspaper that came their way. But she also liked to dream, and sometimes her dreams and thoughts got twisted together and became so real she failed to hear the cry of the baby or the sound of the timber wolves outside.

Along about the tenth or eleventh of February Tom contacted the "granny woman," Aunt Peggy Walters, who lived some three-quarters of a mile away. "Nancy will be needin' you pretty soon," he said. We know the Lincolns had access to a doctor, for when Doctor Daniel B. Potter of Elizabethtown passed away, it was discovered that Tom owed him $1.46. Peggy Walters was summoned because she lived

The Birth Cabin at Hodgenville, Kentucky, where Abraham Lincoln was born on Sunday morning, February 12, 1809.
—Courtesy, Department of Public Information, Frankfort, Kentucky

The building that houses the Birth Cabin at Hodgenville, Kentucky.
—Courtesy, Department of Public Information, Frankfort, Kentucky

nearby, and because a granny woman was considered quite capable of doing the few things that needed to be done.

Tom had plenty of wood for the fire when Peggy Walters pushed through the leather-hinged door on the eleventh. A deeply concerned man, he held Nancy's hand tightly in his own and prayed that every thing would be according to the will of the Lord.

Years later, Peggy Walters told her story. "I was twenty years old, then, and helping to bring a baby into the world was more of an event to me than it became afterward. But I was married young, and had a baby of my own, and I had helped Mother, who, as you know, was quite famous as a granny woman, and I had gone several times to help when I was sent for. It was Saturday afternoon, I remember, when Tom Lincoln sent over and asked me to come, and I got up behind the boy that rode across to fetch me, and I rode across to the cabin that then stood here. It was a short ride, less than a mile. It was winter, but it was mild weather, and I don't think there was any snow. If there was any then, it wasn't much, and no snow fell that night. . . .

"They were poor folks, but so were most of their neighbors, and they didn't lack anything they needed. Nancy had a good feather-bed under her; it wasn't a goose-feather bed, hardly anyone had that kind then, but good hen feathers. And she had blankets enough. There was a little girl there, two years old. Her name was Sarah. She went to sleep before much of anything happened.

"Well, there isn't much a body can tell about things of that kind. Nancy had about as hard a time as most women, I reckon, easier than some and maybe harder than a few. . . . The baby was born about sunup, on Sunday morning . . . .

"Oh, yes, and I remember one other thing. After the baby was born, Tom came and stood beside the bed and looked down at Nancy, lying there so pale and tired, and he stood there with sort of a hang-dog look that a man has, sort of guilty like, but mighty proud, and he says to me, 'Are you sure she's all right, Mis' Walters?' and Nancy kind of stuck out her hand and reached for his, and said, 'Yes, Tom, I'm all right.' And then she said, 'You're glad it's a boy, Tom, aren't you? So am I.' "

When he was certain everything was just as it should be, Tom headed down the road to where the Thomas Sparrows lived. "Nancy's got a baby boy," he said excitedly to Dennis at the door.

Something exciting had happened at last, and so nine-year-old Dennis Hanks took off for the Lincoln cabin, running until he was out of breath.

"What you goin' to name him, Nancy?" he asked after she'd thrown him a tired smile, indicating that he wasn't intruding.

"His name is Abraham," she said proudly. "I've named him after his grandfather."

Years later, Dennis gave his impression of the scene. "Nancy was lyin' thar in a pole bed lookin' purty happy. Tom'd built up a good fire and throwed a b'ar skin over the kivers to keep 'em warm." Then Betsy Sparrow washed the new baby, "put a yaller flannen petticoat an' a linsey shirt on him an' cooked some dried berries with wild honey for Nancy, an' slicked things up an' went home. And that's all the nuss'n either of 'em got."

As Betsy Sparrow left, she promised to come back the next day and do what she could to help.

Dennis, hoping for a playmate, curled up in the bearskin and slept by the fire all night. But his sleep was interrupted by the crying baby and Tom Lincoln pacing back and forth, trying to quiet him. This interruption may have influenced his comments about his new cousin the next day.

After a long, hard look at its drawn legs and clenched fists, Dennis said, "Its skin looks just like red cherry pulp squeezed dry, in wrinkles."

A little bit later, after he'd shyly asked to hold him, Nancy said, "Be keerful, Dennis, fur you air the fust boy he's ever seen."

Gingerly Dennis cradled him in his arms and rocked him back and forth. This was too much for young Abraham. He began to cry and no amount of coaxing would stop him. Pushing the baby over to Betsy Sparrow as if he were ridding himself of the plague, Dennis said, "Aunt, take him! He'll never come to much."

And so it was that while the planets swung wide in their orbits, and a bucket of stars gleamed in union on both the North and the South, on Gettysburg and Chancellorsville, white-lipped Nancy Hanks won her struggle for the new life she was giving to an old world.

That day, those who read the newspapers, read about Thomas Jefferson who was finishing his eighth year as President; of James Madison who was preparing to enter the White House; and of Napoleon's invasion of Spain.

No one then, or for years to come, read about the baby boy who had been born in Tom Lincoln's cabin on the South Fork of Nolin Creek, two and a half miles from Hodgenville. As today, the *real* news of the times did not appear in the newspapers.

In the weeks that followed, while the sounds of the wild squeezed through the single cabin window, Nancy took care of Abraham's every need. Sometimes with a faraway look in her blue-green eyes, she held him close while she rocked back and forth on the back legs of a splint-bottomed chair in front of the fireplace. She often sang him to sleep with the songs of the day. A favorite of hers included this verse:

> "You may bury me in the east,
> You may bury me in the west,
> And we'll ri-ise together in the morning."

Nancy may have hoped that someday he would be elected President, even as other mothers hope their sons will be the President But whether he was elected or not, she was determined that he would know her love.

The cold winds blew hard through the South Fork of Nolin Creek, but they never chilled the love of Nancy Hanks for her son, Abraham.

Nancy Hanks Lincoln State Memorial, Lincoln City, Indiana.
Courtesy, Indiana Department of Conservation

8. KNOB CREEK

Although there were times when Abe and Sarah seemed to have an unwritten agreement to see who could cry the longest and loudest, Nancy was extremely happy. She was deeply in love with Tom, enjoyed William Down's preaching, and had great satisfaction in caring for the family and keeping the cabin clean.

There was no high chair for Sarah. Instead, Nancy turned a chair backwards to the table and Sarah stood on it while she clumsily sought her mouth with the delicious mush and fixin's Nancy prepared. Sometimes Tom brought in honey from a bee tree, or a deer he'd shot, and Nancy made use of it in the best frontier style. She kept her spinning wheel and loom busy and skilfully did the sewing. Sometimes she sewed for the neighbors, for she was known to be an excellent seamstress.

Each day she read the Bible, and as she played hand games with the children and took care of their general needs, she told them about men and women of God who had lived long ago. She spoke of Moses and Paul and Jesus and she spoke with interest and imagination. The routines of life became more regular and she enjoyed them. And then one evening Tom stepped into the cabin with shattering news.

"We've gotta move," he said. His drawl was deliberate, yet firm. "We've gotta move, and we gotta move soon!"

"But Tom, we've already moved three times in only four years! I'm gettin' so I love this place more every day," said Nancy, a sharp knot of disappointment forming in her throat.

"Yes, I know," answered Tom stubbornly. "But we still gotta move. There just ain't no other way!"

"Why?" asked Nancy, going up to him and running rough fingers through his coarse dark hair.

"We gotta move because we don't have a deed to the land. When we bought the farm from Bush we agreed to pay off a lien that was filed against it. Now when I need the deed one of the men involved has moved out of the state. It's all in a big mess and I'm not goin' to wait for the trial or nothin'. I'm gonna move."*

"Is there no other way?" asked Nancy.

"None that I can see," said Tom. Then dropping his voice, he added, "But don't worry. I've found a mighty nice place on Knob Creek. The cabin is right on the Louisville and Nashville turnpike. There's a schoolhouse for Sarah and Abe about two miles from our door, and the creek is plumb full of fish. Just plumb full. What more could a body want?"

And so, after three crop years at Nolin Creek, Tom Lincoln moved his family to Knob Creek. Here he fished, hunted game, worked for others, made coffins and watched his children grow. Dennis Hanks also kept his eye on the growth of Tom's children, especially Abe. Years later Dennis remembered:

"It didn't seem no time till Abe was runnin' 'round in buckskin moccasins an' breeches, a tow-linen shirt an' coonskin cap . . . . Abe never give Nancy no trouble after he could walk except to keep him in clothes. Most of the time we went b'ar foot. . . . Abe was right out in the woods, about as soon as he was weaned, fishin' in the crick . . . . goin' on coon-hunts with Tom an' me an' the dogs; follerin' up bees to find bee-trees, an' drappin' corn fur his pappy. Mighty interestin' life fur a boy, but thar was good many chances he wouldn't live to grow up."

---

*Historians have been puzzled that Tom moved before the case went to court, for the feeling is that he could have paid the lien and kept the land. Three years later the land was sold to John Welsh for $87.74.

Team of horses and wagon in front of Lincoln's boyhood home at Knob Creek.
—Courtesy, Department of Public Information, Frankfort, Kentucky

Knob Creek with its tall trees, wild game, rough pioneers and much-traveled road was like the index page of a dictionary about the raw frontier. As a small boy, Abe studied the index. Later he read the references, and according to subsequent history, he read them and understood them very well. He never forgot Knob Creek and his description of his life there is as vivid as any. "Our farm was composed of three fields which lay in the valley surrounded by high hills and deep gorges. Sometimes when there came a big rain in the hills the water would come down the gorges and spread over the farm. The last thing I remember of doing there was one Saturday afternoon; the other boys planted the corn in what we called 'the big field'—it contained seven acres—and I dropped the pumpkin seed. I dropped two seeds every other hill and every other row. The next Sunday morning there came a big rain in the hills; it did not rain a drop in the valley, but the water, coming down through the gorges, washed ground, corn, pumpkin seeds and all clear off the field."

From those around him, Abe learned that a man who read books was considered to be "eddicated"; that the smoke from the fireplace went up the "chimbly"; and that a blanket was a "kiver."

Nancy was determined that Abe and Sarah learn to read. "I would rather Abe be able to read the Bible than to own a farm if he can't have but one," she said. She also helped teach him to read, using the Bible as a text. Abe soon learned the art, and took his turn reading the Bible at family worship. In addition, he learned to write, a skill his mother never mastered. "It was his custom to form letters," wrote an author in 1900, "to write words wherever he found suitable material. He scrawled them with charcoal, he scored them in the dust, in the sand, in the snow —anywhere and everywhere that lines could be drawn, there he improved his capacity for writing."

Abe and Sarah liked to watch their father as he smoothed boards for the coffins he built. It was great fun to see the long white shavings curl out of the plane and fall to the ground. And then one afternoon two older girls rode up and taught them a thrilling shavings game. The girls selected long shavings, held them at arm's length, closed their eyes, turned around three times and dropped them over their left shoulders. The letter formed by the shaving was the first letter of their future husband's name!

All kinds of people traveled over the turnpike in front of the Lincoln cabin. Little Abe saw rich men, members of Congress and important officials going by in their fine carriages. He also saw gangs of slaves being hastened along by evil-looking masters armed with whips. And he saw the long tracks made by the neighbors as they shuffled through the dust or picked their way over the clinging red mud.

Once on his way home, Abe saw a man in uniform trudging by. When as an adult he was asked if he remembered the War of 1812, Lincoln remembered this man and said: "I had been fishing one day and caught a little fish which I was taking home. I met a soldier in the road, and having always been told at home that we should be good to soldiers, I gave him my fish!"

Nancy was delighted to know about the "subscription" school being conducted by Zachariah Riney. The subscription price was raised and Abe and Sarah were sent. They walked the entire distance each day, and although the round trip was between three and four miles, they never complained. The school was built of logs over a dirt floor.

A reconstructed "Blab School" at Harrodsburg, Kentucky. Sarah and little Abe attended this type of school.
—Photo by Charles Ludwig

There were no windows, and there was only one door. It was called a "blab school" because all the children recited at the same time. While one was saying, "Two times two are four," another might be saying, "Columbus discovered America in 1492."

Riney, their first teacher, was an Irish Catholic; while Caleb Hazel, the next teacher, was a Baptist, attending the same congregation Tom and Nancy attended. These men didn't know much, but they made a sincere effort to transfer all they did know to the children. And, in the main, they were successful.

Along about this time Abe almost drowned, and for the rest of his life Austin Gollaher specialized in telling the story. Here it is in his own words as he related it to a reporter: "Abraham Lincoln and I had been going to school for a year or more, and had become greatly attached to each other. Then school disbanded on account of there being so few scholars, and we did not see each other much for a long while. One Sunday my mother visited the Lincolns, and I was taken along. Abe and I played around all day. Finally, we concluded to cross the creek to hunt for some partridges young Lincoln had seen the day before. The creek was swollen by a recent rain, and, in crossing on the narrow footlog, Abe fell in. Neither of us could swim. I got a long pole and held it out to Abe, who grabbed it. Then I pulled him ashore. He was almost dead, and I was badly scared. I rolled and pounded him in good earnest. Then I got him by the arms and shook him, the water meanwhile pouring out of his mouth. By this means I succeeded in bringing him to, and he was soon all right.

"Then a new difficulty confronted us. If our mothers discovered our wet clothes they would whip us. This we dreaded from experience, and determined to avoid. It was June, the sun was very warm, and we soon dried our clothing by spreading it on the rocks about us. We promised never to tell the story, and I never did until after Lincoln's tragic end."

While the Lincolns lived at Knob Creek, Nancy had a new baby—a boy. She named him Thomas after his father. Sarah and Abe delighted in him, the newest member of the family. But from the very beginning everyone could see that he was not very strong.

Abe used to stand and watch his mother as she rocked the new baby by the fire and prayed that God would send additional strength into the tiny body. "Remember," she would say to those who seemed to question her prayers, "our God is a prayer-hearing God."

9. TROUBLE AND DEATH

Tom Lincoln's love for auctions grew throughout his life. An auction helped the man who was moving, or the widow who was left. It also helped the neighbors who were thus able to get a bargain, and it provided excitement and fellowship. Nancy could usually tell when an auction was due by the gleam in Tom's eyes.

At one auction he bought a wagon for 8½ cents, much to the delight of the children. At another—to the dismay of Nancy—he bought a sword, and at still another he bid in a cow for $9.42. This last purchase made sense and Nancy proceeded to teach Sarah how to milk.

The cow was driven into a corner formed by the fence. Then her calf was released from its pen and allowed to start its breakfast. About the time the milk started to flow properly, the calf was gently returned to its pen, and then the master of ceremonies directed the milk into a gourd gingerly held in one hand. This gourd was emptied from time to time in a nearby bucket. Finally, when there was still a little milk left, the calf was allowed to return and finish its meal. Milking stools were seldom if ever used in those days.

Soon little Thomas became so ill a doctor was called. With their hands tightly gripped, Tom and Nancy stood by as their baby struggled for life. They prayed and hoped and worked, but without success. In time the breathing stopped and all signs of pulse vanished. Tom closed its eyes and laid a penny on each one so they would stay closed. The death of a baby in those days was very common. There were few families that had not lost at least one. But this was *their* baby, and they were brokenhearted.

Tom made a little coffin, which Nancy lovingly padded

The Lincoln Cabin at Knob Creek. It was here Little Tom died.
—Photo by Charles Ludwig

with cotton and lined with fresh cloth she had just woven. The body was laid inside, and then after each member of the family had had a last look, Tom put the lid on and pegged it tight.

Burial was on Muldraugh's Hill. There was no funeral sermon or ceremony of any kind. Some time later, while the red earth on the grave-mound was still fresh, a limestone marker with the initials T.L. chiseled in it was placed at the head.

Tom and Nancy may have hoped that they could live out their days at Knob Creek, but once again they were faced with the problem of land titles—a problem that plagued many in Kentucky in those days. This time a suit was brought against Tom and nine of his neighbors by the Thomas Middleton heirs, who claimed that their farms were part of a tract of 10,000 acres that Middleton had acquired in 1786. According to this claim, Lincoln, LaFollette, Brownfield, Tucker and all the others were trespassers—that even though they had paid down money they did not own their land.

Tom and Nancy were staggered by the blow. But after visiting with some neighbors, Tom decided to fight his case in court. He employed Worden Pope, one of the best land attorneys in Kentucky, to defend him. Then on May 13, 1816, Tom received an order from the court with an additional annoyance. The order decreed "that Thomas Lincoln be and he is hereby appointed surveyor of that part of the road leading from Nolin to Bardstown which lies between the Bigg hill (Muldraugh's) and the Rolling Fork in place of George Redman and that all the hands that assisted said Redman to assist said Lincoln in keeping said road in repair."

This was a job that no one wanted. It was a kind of tax, and most people tried to avoid the responsibility. Indeed, it was so unpopular the law threatened the sheriff with a fine if he didn't notify the chosen surveyor of his obligation. And the surveyor was in jeopardy of a $2.50 to $10.00 fine if he failed "to perform his duty agreeably to law."

Along about this time, letters began to drift into Kentucky about the wonderful land in Indiana. These letters and stories were as thrilling to Tom Lincoln as Daniel Boone's descriptions had been to his father a generation before. Indiana was about to become a state. A constitution had been drafted in June, and the first election was carried out in August.

That year the Boston *Gazette* was quoted by the Vincennes *Western Star* as having said: "Probably no country ever progressed so rapidly in population and improvement as our own western states and territories have in the last ten years. . . . Even Indiana, which we had hardly learnt to consider anything but a pathless wilderness, has risen to the magnitude of a state, her population having increased from 30 to 60,000."*

All of these events provided a temptation too powerful for Tom Lincoln to resist. "Nancy," he said, "we're goin' to move to Indiana. I've put up with bad land titles long enough. Titles are sure on the other side of the Ohio. At least I'm gonna go over and investigate."

While Tom went on his journey to spy out the land, Nancy remained at home with the children. In the depths of her heart she hoped they could remain in Kentucky with their friends and relatives. This would be their fourth move, and she was agreed with others that three moves were as bad as a fire. But as an obedient wife, she knew she would have to obey, and this she would do most gladly.

During the nights while Tom was away she sat by the fire, read her Bible and prayed. Her constant petition was

*This interesting quotation was turned up by Louis A. Warren in his excellent book: *Lincoln's Youth*.

that God would have His way and that she would be a useful servant. Little Abe and Sarah were a constant inspiration. She hoped that God would use them somehow in His work.

10. PIGEON CREEK

Tom Lincoln's heart continued to churn with enthusiasm all the way back from Indiana. He had seen the new country and old Kentucky friends who had migrated before told him of the greatness of the tall-timbered land.

"There will be free education for Abe and Sarah!" he said to Nancy, his grey eyes bright with excitement. "And slavery isn't allowed. There ain't narry a slave in the whole country. Titles can be registered at Vincennes and they're plumb sure. There won't be no chance of losin' the land again. And besides, land is cheap—real cheap!"

Near where the present city of Gentryville stands, Tom had reserved a quarter of a section of choice land. There, in Hurricane Township in Perry County, he had reverently marked out his land with a large pile of brush at each corner. Tom felt he had chosen well, for there were springs on the land and the little Pigeon Creek meandered by just a little to the north. Having an adequate supply of fresh water was more than half the battle.

Reuben Grigsby, whom Tom had met on the trail near the present city of Santa Claus, Indiana, had a farm near the one he had chosen. He turned out to be a most agreeable man. He leased eight acres to Tom for three years, promised him a job making barrels, and helped him throw together a temporary home where Nancy and the children could stay until a cabin could be erected.

Tom sold his contested rights to the Knob Creek farm and prepared to move to Indiana. But before leaving, there were many things that had to be done. It would be impossible to take with them all the "house plunder" they had accumulated in their ten years of married life. Moreover, it would be foolish to haul such things as tables and chairs when new ones could be made in Indiana with hardly any trouble at all. This meant an auctioneer had to be summoned, a task Tom thoroughly enjoyed.

We know that Tom was baptized while he lived at Knob Creek. Whether it was at this time or previously we have no way of knowing. We can, however, be certain that he was immersed, for he was a Baptist. The chances are that this was done by William Downs in Knob Creek.

Although the new farm would be less than one hundred miles away, it would take nearly a week to get there, and there was no easy way to keep in contact with old friends and relatives. The mails were slow and uncertain. Moreover, few people could read, and even less could write. Knowing this, Tom and Nancy visited their kinfolk for a parting meal and final word. And then, once again, they climbed the dreary path up Muldraugh's Hill to spend a last moment of meditation at the grave of little Tom.

Nancy's eyes were still wet when she returned to the loaded wagon standing by the cabin. It was mighty hard to leave Kentucky where her roots had been deepening since her infancy. Her relatives, too, hated to see her go. And so, as was the custom in those days, they followed the wagon for a way. This helped make parting easier.

No one knows, of course, what was taken along. But we can be sure that Nancy was not willing to part with her spinning wheel or loom; and Tom insisted on taking his tools and the pots and pans they had been collecting through the years. Some recalled that the wagon was drawn by horses, and since Tom was taxed for several horses that year, this is probably true. Also, we can be sure that at least one cow tagged on behind.

Did they stop at E-town on the way? Probably, for it was on the way and would give the family opportunity to bid farewell to some more friends.

The great time for Sarah and Abe was when they came to the half-a-mile-wide Ohio. Tom drove the wagon slowly

An old illustration of Tom Lincoln crossing the Ohio River on the move to Pigeon Creek, Indiana.
—Photo by Charles Ludwig

along the Ohio until he was at the ferry landing just north of Hawesville at a spot directly across from the mouth of the Anderson Creek on the Indiana side. There he waited until Hugh Thompson arrived with his ferry. The fare on his big flat boat had been set by law. A horse and wagon was charged $1.00; a man and a horse, 25 cents; great cattle, 12½ cents; foot passengers, 12½ cents. Children under ten were carried free.

As Nancy stepped with the children into the boat she felt an instinctive urge to stay with them. Neglecting them for even a brief moment could mean that they might fall into the muddy, rolling river. At a time of excitement there was no tellin' what Abe and Sarah might do!

Tom and his family stepped ashore in Indiana almost on the day Indiana was taken into the Union as the nineteenth state—December 11, 1816. At the point of landing they were still some sixteen miles from their destination. But these last miles were not as difficult as they might have been, for the road overseers had had strict orders "to open a road from Troy to the Hurricane, 12 feet wide, in such manner that carriages can conveniently pass and that they have the same completed by next November court."

The way into the farm was not so easy, for it was virgin land. When the wagon finally squeaked to a stop near the shelter Tom and Reuben Grigsby had built, Nancy was profoundly happy. The shed-like affair was made of poles and was approximately twenty feet long and sixteen feet wide. The southeast side was completely open, its only wall being the log fire Tom kindled.

"Well, here we are," said Tom, after he'd brought in the pots and pans. "We're in a new land and God is gonna bless us."

Nancy cooked the supper that night over an open fire. If she was disappointed by what she saw she didn't say so. Faithful as ever, she prepared a place for Sarah and Abe to sleep and then she got out her Bible. "Remember our God is a prayer-hearing God," she said, "and He is with us right here in Indiana. My hope is that we'll always be faithful in followin' and trustin' Him."

That night as the howls of the wolves, the shrill screams of the panthers and the snap of the burning logs filled the shed, Nancy was glad she had committed all her ways to the Lord.

The Lord was faithful—always!

11. CHURCH

By the time her first Sunday in Indiana had come around, Nancy was delighted to learn that a Baptist church had been organized in the community. And, better still, that Thomas Downs, a brother of William Downs, pastor of their old church in Kentucky, had helped organize it. Although the congregation had no meeting house at the time, a careful book of minutes was kept. The minutes of the founding meeting on June 8, 1816, read:

"First the church chose B (ro.) Samuel Bristow, moderrater and Thomas Downs clak for the meeting. 2. invited Brethern of sister churches to seat with us . . . ." After this eleven articles of faith were listed:

"1. we believe in one god the Father the word & the holley gost who haith created all things that are created by the word of his power for his pleasure.

"2. we believe the old & new testaments are the words of god thare are everry thing contained thare in nessarssary for mans Salvation & rule of faith and pracktice.

"7. we believe that Good works are the fruits of Grace and follow after Justification.

"8. we believe that babtism and the Lord's supper are ordenances of Jesus Christ and that true believers are the onely proper subjects and the only proper mode of babtism is immertion.

"9. we believe the washing of feet is a command to be complide with when opportunity serves . . . ."*

The Lincolns began to attend the services immediately, wherever they were conducted in the various cabins. Nevertheless, they did not join at this time. The reason for

*The original copy of this book is in the Illinois State Historical Library in Springfield.

this may have been that their church in Kentucky had no written creed, while this one did.

The services were strictly evangelical. Upon entering a place of worship, the men and women immediately separated, each group going to a set of hard benches reserved for them. The men "saints" sat on one side of the aisle and the women saints sat on the other side. Non-members sat in the middle section toward the center aisle on benches known as "the sinners' seats."

The congregations loved to sing. Favorite hymns were: "Am I a Soldier of the Cross?" "There Is a Fountain Filled with Blood," "How Tedious and Tasteless the Hours," and "Alas, and Did My Saviour Bleed?"

The sermons were long and repetitious. But even though many of the preachers could barely read, some of them were very eloquent. Young Abe especially liked the arm-swinging kind, and later in the years of his fame, he said that he liked to hear preachers preach as if "they were fighting bees."

A note that often appeared in the sermon was that of predestination, the preacher declaring "God knew you would be here before you came to church today."

After the last point in the sermon, the preacher would pause and in a low tone would ask, "Any enquiry after peace and fellowship in the church?" He would then wait for a moment and if no one said anything, he would add: "Nothing of that nature? How beautiful it is to dwell in peace and harmony." Next the people would get up and file toward the pulpit while they continued to sing. There, they would shake hands with the speaker, and then with each other on their way out.

This group of Baptists believed in supporting their ministers, for one of their adopted articles of faith read: "we belive that no minister ought to preach the gospel that is not calld and sent of god and they ought to be proven by hiering them & and we allow of none to preach Amongst us but such as are well recommended And that we aurght to Contribute to him who Faithfully Labors Amongst us in word and Docttrin...."

Many of the visiting preachers visited the Lincolns, and some of them spent the night. Young Abe liked to question them in order to learn all that he could from their experience. On one of these occasions Abe turned to the preacher. "Who was the father of Zebedee's children?" he asked.

Astonished by such a question, the minister mumbled, "I don't know."

Abe, however, appreciated these preachers and any ignorance they displayed was neutralized by Nancy's vital and radiant faith. A lady, visiting the White House during Lincoln's administration, wrote, "It was his custom when waiting for lunch to take his mother's old, worn-out Bible and lie on the lounge and read, and one day he asked me what book I liked to read best, and I said, 'I am fond of the Psalms.' 'Yes,' said he to me, 'they are the best, for I find in them something for every day in the week.'"

He listened closely to the sermons, and on one occasion he astonished his friends by standing on a stump and repeating Jeremiah Cash's text and complete sermon. He even remembered the gestures, which he imitated with a generous flourish. After Nancy's death, and after Abe's father had remarried, his stepsister, Matilda Johnson, remembered that sometimes when her mother could not attend the services, "Abe would take down the Bible, read a verse, give out a hymn and we would sing. He would preach and we would do the crying. Sometimes he would join in the chorus of tears."

John G. Nicolay, President Abraham Lincoln's private secretary, wrote that Abe "... praised the simplicity of the Gospels. He often declared that the Sermon on the Mount contained the essence of all law and justice, and that the

Lord's Prayer was the sublimest composition in human language."

Nicolay also recalled: "He could repeat from memory whole chapters of Isaiah, the New Testament and the Psalms."

The little congregation grew, and the cabins became much too small to hold the crowds. The members began to talk about building a meeting house where everyone could meet in comfort and with plenty of room. Finally a choice lot was selected a little over a mile southwest of Tom's farm on the Buckhorn Creek. Then the congregation appointed various ones to help with the work. David Turnham made brick for the chimney. Reuben Grigsby, Sr., James Gentry, Jacob and Robert Oskins and others were given the job of cutting down and preparing logs. Noah Gordon agreed to hew the timbers. Tom Lincoln was voted boss carpenter.

The completed building was a story and a half high, thirty feet long and twenty-six feet wide. A chimney stood at each end and there was a large fireplace for warmth during the winter. The bench on which the preachers sat was long enough to hold six at a time, and it was frequently filled, for the various churches liked to get together.

Tom Lincoln built the pulpit of solid cherry. It had to be strong to withstand the oratorical pounding of the preachers!

On June 12, 1823, Thomas Lincoln was given the job of trustee, an office he shared with Reuben Grigsby and William Barker. Abe was made janitor. This we know, because years after the building was abandoned, someone climbed into the loft and found "in a crevice between two upper logs an old faded memorandum book." One of the entries read:

"Dr. To 1 broom
To ½ doz tallow candles."

It was signed, "Abe Lincoln, Sexton."

An old illustration showing President Abraham Lincoln near Tom and Nancy's log cabin at Pigeon Creek.
—Courtesy, Library of Congress

12. THE CABIN

Each day the howling winds and swirling smoke reminded Nancy that a permanent cabin would soon have to be built. Fortunately Tom was an experienced cabin builder, having built two or three of his own, and perhaps several for other people. The new land was covered with magnificent oak, hickory, walnut, maple and black cherry, and so Nancy didn't have to complain much in order to get things started.

After the site had been chosen, some forty logs, a foot thick, were selected and dragged to the little clearing. Then sixteen of these logs were trimmed and cut so that they were approximately twenty feet long. Eight were for the front. Eight were for the back. Next, sixteen logs, eighteen feet long, were prepared for the end walls. Finally, four large, flat stones were brought up to become the corner supports.

The logs were then carefully notched and fitted tightly together. The outside walls completed, smaller logs were cut for the loft where Abe would sleep. A door and window were sawed in, and then half-inch thick clapboards were prepared for a gently-sloping roof.

A huge fireplace was laid at one end and a thick chimney, standing on the outside, was erected. The next job was one in which Abe and Sarah were able to help. This was the task of closing the cracks between the logs, for no two logs were absolutely straight. Tom cut a tall pile of narrow wedges and drove them solidly between the crevices. Then Abe and Sarah made big gobs of clay, which they pushed into the leaks the wedges didn't quite fill. It was exciting work, and they filled both the inside and the outside walls. Shutting out the winter and fierce winds was not an easy job.

The final job was to pound long pegs into the logs leading to Abe's loft. They had to be wide enough for his feet and strong enough not to break when he put his full weight on them. And his weight was increasing enormously every day.

The floor, like the one at Nolin Creek, was of packed dirt. Nancy viewed the completed cabin with a critical eye, and then proceeded to arrange her furniture until the room was snug and comfortable. By placing a bearskin here, deer horns there, a pumpkin in the corner, braided corn on the rafters, and her cooking utensils by the fireplace, she changed the place from a cabin into a home.

One of the jobs Nancy assigned to Abe and Sarah was that of carrying water. The woods in those days were filled with game. Passenger pigeons by the thousands flew by, Carolina parakeets chirped in the trees, and various animals frequented the salt licks on the Lincoln property. Getting the water in the daylight was not so hard, but sometimes when they had to go at dusk their hearts beat in terror, and the stories the neighbors told about ghosts didn't help matters.

Just after the cabin was completed a flock of wild turkeys settled near the cabin.

"Pap isn't home, Ma," said Abe, looking at the big birds hungrily. "Would it be all right if I shot one with his gun?"

"But do you know how to shoot a gun?" she asked.

"I've seen Pap shoot it."

"All right, then. But be keerful."

Slowly Abe pushed the long barrel through a crack in the wall, took careful aim and pulled the trigger. The gun exploded with a roar, walloping him on the shoulder until he nearly fell. But when the smoke cleared he found his aim had been true, for there was a big turkey flopping out in the yard. Looking at the dead bird filled him with both joy and remorse. He decided right then never to shoot another bird or animal.

The whole Pigeon Creek area was devastated time and again by bears. These marauders not only killed the livestock, but occasionally molested the people as well. Sometimes, when the farmers had had enough of it, they would organize an extensive hunt. On one of these hunts nine bears were brought in.

All of this made a deep impression on Abe. In 1846 he described a bear hunt in a long poem—a poem that shows he had considerable literary talent. Here are three of the verses:

> "At top of speed, the horse-men come,
>   All screaming in a row.
> 'Whoop! Take him Tiger. Seize him Drum.'
>   Bang,—bang—the rifles go.
>
> "And furious now, the dog he tears,
>   And crushes in his ire.
> Wheels right and left, and upwards rears,
>   With eyes of burning fire.
>
> "But leaden death is at his heart,
>   Vain all the strength he plies.
> And, spouting blood from every part,
>   He reels, and sinks, and dies."

Being large for his age, Abe started using an ax when he was only eight. The farm had to be cleared and Abe had the job of cutting down the thick undergrowth while his father attacked the bigger trees. Tom also showed him how to hack a deep circle around a larger tree so that it would die and be easier to cut down and destroy later.

Coming home with blistered hands, sore muscles and an empty stomach, Abe was ready for the hog and hominy, fried bear, corn bread, or whatever else Nancy may have prepared. Sometimes he was so hungry he could hardly wait for his father to say grace.

After Tom had cleared much of his land and had raised a crop, he kissed Nancy goodbye and headed for the United States Land Office at Vincennes, sixty miles away. On his joyous return he showed Nancy Receipt No. 8499, which was dated October 15, 1817, and handed to him by Receiver Nathaniel Ewing. It was addressed to: "Thomas Linkern of Perry County, Indiana," and acknowledged payment of $16 for a "deposit on account of Land for which he intends to apply."

The following December after a second trip to Vincennes he showed Nancy another receipt that said: "The sum of sixty four dollars which with the sum of Sixteen Dollars heretofore paid by him, per receipt No. 8499 dated the 15th of October 1817 is in full the first installment of the purchase of the S. W. qt. Section No. 32 in township No. 4 S of Range 5 w."

These legal receipts gave Nancy a new confidence. They meant she wouldn't have to move again.

13. SCHOOL AND NEIGHBORS

In the fall of 1817 the Lincolns welcomed unexpected company. Losing their land in Kentucky over a faulty title, Thomas and Betsy Sparrow had decided to move to Pigeon Creek.

The Lincolns extended their hospitality and helped them to move into their old temporary house. "When you're settled and have learned the lay of the land," said Tom, "you can get a farm of your own and we'll help you build a cabin."

Dennis Hanks had moved with them, and Abe was delighted. He had never had a finer playmate than his cousin. Often when he pulled his bearskin over him at night his mind had gone back to Kentucky. Now Dennis was by his side. In a moment he began to show him around. He pointed out the place where he had downed the turkey; led him to the spot where the latest bear had been killed; and told him about his favorite fishing holes. The two became almost as close as David and Jonathan. And Abe never forgot Dennis, even in the days of his greatness.

Living to an old age, Dennis Hanks became a colorful source of information for Lincoln scholars. In an interview with Eleanor Atkinson, Dennis said: "I went down to Washington to see Abe, an' thar he was with a big watch an' chain spread over his wescoat. I plagued him about bein' so fine, an' he sez: 'Denny, I bet you'd carry a watch if you had one, you old coon.' He went out and bought this fur me and I've carried it ever sence. Ain't many folks ever gits to see it. Thar's a feller up in Chicago that's plumb crazy over Abe, and he offered me five hundred dollars fur it . . . ."

When Nancy learned there was a blab school within

walking distance of their cabin, she enrolled Abe and Sarah at once. Their first teacher was probably Andrew Crawford who was also a justice of the peace. A search of the records show that he performed many marriage ceremonies for members of the Pigeon Creek community. As in backwoods Kentucky, very little education was required of a teacher. If they were able to teach "readin', writin', and cipherin' to the Rule of Three," they were considered qualified.

William E. Barton was acquainted with this kind of school and so his description can be considered accurate: "The schoolhouses were bare, log buildings, with the cracks unchinked. They were built on slopes high enough at one end for hogs to rest under the floor, and fill the place with fleas. . . . The benches were of puncheon and had no backs. . . . But the children departed from these schools less ignorant than when they entered."[*]

This description may explain an experience Abe is supposed to have had about this time. Knocking timidly at the door of Shadrach Hall, a tanner who lived some four miles away, he was invited in by the man's son, Wesley, a boy about Abraham's age.

"Mother sent me to borrow your fine-toothed comb," Abe mumbled to Mrs. Hall.

"What's the matter?" she enquired curiously.

"Mother thinks we got the creepers!"

Mrs. Hall spread a paper on the floor and combed out the hair of both of the boys. And as she combed, the paper filled with creepers, much to the horror of everyone.

One of the books the children studied was the *Dilworth Speller,* first published by Thomas Dilworth in England in 1740. This book went out of its way to tack on a moral to every story and list of words. Wishing to use a set of

[*]*The Life of Abraham Lincoln,* p. 121

words with three letters or less, the following sentences were included:

> "No man may put off the law of God."
> "The way of God is no ill way."
> "My joy is in God all the day."
> "A bad man is a foe of God."

The Bible was also used as a reader, and an experience at school while reading it provided Abe with one of his best stories. The children were reading the story of Nebuchadnezzar and the golden image from the third chapter of Daniel. One of the readers was an under-sized boy by the name of Bud who had never learned to read well. "Little Bud stumbled on Shadrach, floundered on Meshach, and went all to pieces on Abed-nego. Instantly the hand of the master dealt him a cuff on the side of the head and left him wailing and blubbering as the next boy in line took up the reading. But before the girl at the end of the line had done reading he had subsided into sniffles and finally became quiet. His blunder and disgrace were forgotten by the other members of the class until his turn was approached to read again. Then, like a thunderclap out of a clear sky, he set up a wail which even alarmed the master, who with rather unusual gentleness, inquired, 'What's the matter now?'

"Pointing with a shaking finger at the verse which a few moments later would fall to him to read, Bud managed to quaver out the answer:

"'Look there marster,' he cried, 'there comes them same three fellers again.'"

Abe was an excellent speller and generally won the spelling matches. But he could also be gracious and helpful to others. At one of the matches, Mr. Crawford gave out the word *defied*. As each youngster attempted it they used a *y* instead of an *i*. This infuriated Crawford until, almost beside himself, he half-shouted, "I'll keep you here all night if you don't spell that word correctly!"

Abe knew that many of the children would be whipped if they got home late. This, he couldn't tolerate. Presently it was Katy Robey's turn. Lincoln was a little sweet on her, and this gave him added incentive to be helpful.

"D-e-f," she began, her voice raw with terror. "D-e-f-"

Instantly Abe got her attention with a broad wink, and slyly pointed to his eye.

This was all the help she needed. "D-e-f-i-e-d," she concluded promptly.

Relieved, Crawford dismissed the class at once.

Back at the cabin, Abe and Sarah studied their speller and the Bible by the light of the fire. When they came to such a sentence as: "It is a commendable thing for a boy to apply his mind to the study of good letters; they will always be useful to him: they will procure him the love and favor of good men, which those that are wise value more than riches and pleasure," Nancy would attempt to explain it for them. She also drilled them in their spelling.

Abe got hold of *Aesop's Fables* and the *Arabian Nights* and pored over them by the hour. Dennis remembered: "Abe'd lay on his stummick by the fire, an' read out loud to me 'n' Aunt Sairy, an' we'd laugh when he did.... I reckon Abe read the book [*Arabian Nights*] a dozen times, an' knowed them yarns by heart."

One of the yarns made a special impression on him. "One I ricollect was about a feller that got near some ... fool rocks 'at drawed all the nails out o' his boat an' he got a duckin'."

Dennis disapproved the stories, warmly declaring the *Arabian Nights* was "a pack of lies."

Sometimes when it was very late and Abe wanted to continue reading, he lit his carrot lamp—a carrot hollowed out, filled with lard and provided with a wick. Tom Lincoln could not understand the purpose of all this reading, but Nancy always stood up for Abe.

Many of the neighbors in the Pigeon Creek community were as interesting as the stories in the books, and Abe used to question Nancy about them. Reuben Grigsby, for example, had a limp and often acted like an Indian. A little investigation revealed that when Reuben was four years old a group of sun-worshiping Indians swooped down on the Grigsby home in Bardstown, Kentucky. Since the father was away, Reuben and the family were helpless.

In desperation Reuben hid in the stick-and-mud chimney, but not being able to keep his feet out of sight, he was pulled down by a painted brave and was forced to stand and watch while his three brothers and a sister were killed. The Indians then picked him up and as they carried him, forced his mother with a baby in her arms to go along with them.

When Mrs. Grigsby tired and lagged behind, they impatiently killed her and dashed the baby's head against a tree. Then they tossed Reuben into a river. But an old squaw who had taken a fancy to him waded out into the water and rescued him. Again they threw him in, and again she rescued him. This time it was agreed she could have him.

Reuben continued to live with the Indians until he was eleven. During this time he developed the "white swelling." A squaw treated his leg with herb poultices, nevertheless it did not grow to the size of the other leg and this accounted for his limp.

His life with the Indians explained his strange ways and long silences.

The Turnhams, Whitmans, Carters, Wrights, Hardins and others all had their peculiar stories and Nancy heard them all, for it was almost impossible to keep a family secret on Pigeon Creek.

Needing some flour, Abe's mother gave him a sack of

corn and sent him over to Noah Gordon's horse mill one and a quarter miles to the south. Here, the customers were obliged to pour their own corn into the hopper and then hitch their own horse to the long driving sweep that supplied the power.

Finding a long line of people ahead, Abe was forced to wait. This made him uncomfortable. He passed the time by watching the wooden cogs and the big stones as they turned. Turning to his friend, David Turnham, he remarked: "My hound pup can eat all the meal that thing'll grind in a day and then howl for his supper."

Finally, near dusk, Abe's turn came. He hitched up his mare and urged her to start going. But she didn't go fast enough to suit him. He swatted her with a whip and yelled, "Get up!" But the mare, too, was impatient. She retaliated with a swift kick that caught Abe smack on the forehead and sent him sprawling to the ground.

Gordon threw down his toll box with which he had been dipping out the mill's share of the flour and stopped everything.

Blood poured from Abe's mouth and nose and one of the wide-eyed onlookers shouted, "He's killed! He's killed!" David Turnham ran all the way to the Lincoln cabin and returned in a wagon with Tom. The community swarmed in with advice and help. Some suggested a cold cloth on his forehead; others that he be given some raw whisky; and others that he be bled a little.

The crowd showed its concern by staying up all night. In the morning Abe suddenly opened his eyes, causing one neighbor to shout, "Look! He's coming back to life!"

"He's coming straight from the dead!" added another, cocking his head to one side.

Abe's body began to jerk, and then he finished the sentence the mare had interrupted with her hoof. "You old hussy!" he exclaimed.

In 1818 it was voted to take a part of Perry County and

a part of Warrick County and develop a new division, which was named Spencer County in honor of Spier Spencer who had been killed at the Battle of Tippecanoe. Rockport was named the county seat. This meant the Lincoln farm was now in Carter Township in Spencer County. Nevertheless, Tom and Nancy's land was secure. In this, they rejoiced.

A diorama of "Lincoln's Indiana Home, 1824." The woman in the background is Sarah Bush Lincoln, Abe's stepmother.
—Courtesy, Chicago Historical Society

14. SORROW

When it was announced at the Lincoln table that one of the cows had the trembles, there was a complete silence during which Tom and Nancy exchanged long, terrified glances. An atmosphere of gloom settled over the cabin. But before either Abe or Sarah could ask the questions that were forming on their faces, Tom expressed the gravity of the situation by lowering his head and slowly muttering, " 'Tis the heavy hand of Providence laid upon me. Whom the Lord loveth He chasteneth."

"This means that we should not drink any milk," said Nancy. "If the cow really has the trembles it's poisoned. One drink and you're dead." The look of concern deepened in her angular face. "Unless I'm mistaken the milk sickness has come to Pigeon Creek and there will be funerals—many, many funerals!"

"Does this mean we're goin' to die?" asked eleven-year-old Sarah.

"I—I don't know," said Nancy thoughtfully. "But I do know that our God is a prayer-hearing God. We must all begin to pray, and we must all be prepared to go if we're called...."

Twenty-two years later the Providence, Rhode Island, *Journal* carried an article explaining the terror to its eastern readers: "There is no announcement which strikes the members of a western community with so much dread as the report of a case of milk sickness .... No emigrant enters a region of southern Indiana, Illinois or Western Kentucky to locate himself without first making inquiry if the milk sickness was ever known there .... I have passed many a deserted farm where the labors of the emigrant had prepared for himself and family a comfortable home surrounded with ample corn and wheat field, and inquired the reason of its abandonment, and learned that milk sickness had frightened away its tenants and depopulated the neighborhood...."

Each day Nancy went about her chores hoping there would be no outbreak of the disease, that the cow was suffering from something other than the trembles. It was a vain hope. The cow died having every evidence of the scourge. And then there was a sound on the step and the door flew open.

"Uncle Thomas is sick," panted Dennis Hanks, "Aunt Betsy thinks he's plumb got it...."

Although neighbors warned that she was risking her life, Nancy could not stay from a neighbor in need—especially one like Thomas Sparrow who had raised her.

Thomas had every symptom of the disease. His temperature went down; he became extremely thirsty; started to vomit, was dizzy; his breathing became erratic, and his breath putrid. Each day he complained of sharp pains in his legs and became weaker. Nancy asked Sarah to help care for Tom and Abe while she nursed her uncle.

The nearest doctor was thirty-five miles away, and even if he had been available he could have done little good. Sometimes when the doctors were confronted with the disease, they bled the victims with a lancet and fed them tea made of corn husks, but always with little success. The disease was not understood in those days. Now we know it was caused by drinking the milk of a cow that had fed on snake root—*Eupatorium Urticaefolium*—a tall plant that still grows in southern Indiana, and that is filled with a poisonous substance, Tremetol.

On September 21, Thomas knew that his time was short. Realizing that he had never prepared a will, he summoned Nancy and Thomas Carter to his side and dictated one. All the property was to go to Betsy and after her death "the whole property is to fall to Dennis Hanks when he comes of age."

Nancy signed as a witness with her mark.

In a few days Betsy also died, having succumbed to the same disease.

Tom Lincoln made a coffin for each of them and stood silently with Nancy as they were lowered into their graves in a little clearing some fifteen hundred feet to the south of the Lincoln cabin.

Putting an arm around the grieving Dennis, Nancy said, "Now that Tom and Betsy are gone you must come and live with us. What we have is yours . . . ."

Dennis was thankful for the invitation and moved in at once, and Abe was glad to have him. Next Mrs. Peter Brooner was stricken. Again Nancy followed the dark forest paths to the home of a neighbor and ministered to her. But again the disease could not be stopped. Mrs. Brooner passed away during the night of September 28.

Without a request, Tom made another coffin and stood again with Nancy as it was lowered into a grave next to those of Tom and Betsy Sparrow.

And then as she worked in the cabin Nancy began to reel. A sour taste formed in her mouth and deep pains struck at her limbs. She climbed into her pole bed and summoned Tom. "I think I've got it," she whispered.

Tom closed his eyes and prayed and fought back the tears that rushed to the surface.

By this time Nancy knew all of the symptoms. There could be no mistake about it. She had the milk sick! She looked at nine-year-old Abe reading by the fire and watched little Sarah washing the dishes. They were at a point in life when they especially needed a mother. "Oh, God," she prayed daringly, "if it be Thy will . . . ."

That night as Nancy groaned and twisted on her bed, Abe and Dennis slept together in the loft. Abe could hear the dull crunch of the corn husks as his mother turned on the mattress. The sound both comforted and frightened him. Once or twice he heard her murmur, "Tom, you must pray. Remember our God is a prayer-hearing God. . . ."

In the days that followed Nancy worsened and William Wood, a neighbor, came over and sat up all night so Tom could get some sleep.

Nancy's dark skin became sallow. Her blue-green eyes lost their luster and receded deep within their sockets. Then she was seized with a fit of vomiting. This was the last stage and she knew it. She motioned Abe over to her side.

"I am going away from you and I shall not return," she said softly, speaking slowly and with great effort. "I know you will be a good boy. Be kind to Sarah and your father. I want you to live as I have taught you and to love your heavenly Father."

Abe listened carefully and pushed tight fists into his eyes in an effort to dam up the tears. But his fists weren't big enough to stop the flood. They spilled down his cheeks and fell to the dirt floor and disappeared. Soon Nancy closed her eyes and was still, and Abe was made to know that his mother had started on her far journey. The date was October 5, 1818. It was a date and scene Abe was never to forget.

Once again Tom got out his whipsaw to make the necessary coffin. This time he selected a black cherry log that had been left over from the temporary pole house he and Grigsby had built for their first dwelling in Indiana. It was a part of something he and Nancy had shared and was a profound symbol of their love . . . .

From vast experience Tom knew how to mark and cut the boards and to smooth them with his jack-plane. But this time his tears made it difficult to see the marks. Abe and Sarah watched the long wide shavings curl out of the plane with no desire at all to play their old shavings game. Their world had suddenly lost its glamour.

"I'll be needin' some pegs, Abe," said Tom. "Pick up

some short pieces of cherry wood from the pile over there and start whittlin' 'em fur me."

Abe selected the best pieces he could find, and then sitting in the doorway he began to cut them with his pocketknife. Some neighbor women were on the inside preparing the body. As he worked, he kept glancing their way. And each time he turned back to his work, he was determined to make the pegs as fine as possible. It was the last thing he could do for his mother.

The women placed the body inside the coffin. Each one had a last look, and then Tom placed the lid on top and drove the pegs into their sockets. Reuben Grigsby had kindly brought over his ox-drawn sled. The coffin was gently lifted over the runners and secured in the center. And then the procession started on its way to the clearing where Nancy would be laid near the others who had so recently made their departure.

The golden, brown, yellow, and rust-colored leaves of the trees were falling as the sled moved slowly over the wilderness trail Nancy knew so well. The leaves were soft and gentle and beautiful and the smell of the damp woods filled the air. Birds circled and fluttered above and their shadows moved across the sled.

Abe was speechless, as through his tears he saw his mother being lowered into the grave opened next to that of Mrs. Brooner, and as he heard the thud of the dirt falling on the smooth, black cherry lid. He remembered the pegs and he was glad he had made them so well. After the grave was filled, he saw Peter Brooner reach across the swollen mound, grasp his father's hand in a firm grip, and heard him say, "Now we are brothers."

Tom only answered with a nod, for the lump in his throat wouldn't allow a word to get by.

The housework was now piled on Sarah's shoulders. She did the best she could, but it was hard to keep up with the high standards set by Nancy. Dennis Hanks remembered those days very well. "Sairy was a little gal, only 'leven, and she'd git so lonesome, missin' her mother, she'd sit by the fire and cry. Me 'n' Abe got 'er a baby coon an' a turtle, and tried to git her a fawn but we couldn't ketch any."

As the months moved slowly by, Abe kept thinking of his mother. Maybe there was something else he could yet do for her—something that would fix the memory of her kindness into the minds of the community. Then a bold thought took possession of him.

He got a sheet of paper, and dipping a turkey-feather pen into some ink he and Dennis had made of blackberry briar roots, addressed a letter to Reverend David Elkins. He asked the minister if he could find a way to come to Pigeon Creek and preach a funeral sermon over the grave of his mother and the graves of her friends.

Elkins was a big man. He weighed over two hundred and sported long red hair and a full beard of red whiskers. Before his conversion at twenty-two he was famous as a two-fisted fighter, whisky drinker, fiddler and tough. He went by the name of Devil Dave and it was claimed he could lick his weight in wildcats.

He never learned to read. The only writin' he could recognize was the letter "O"—and that was because of its simple shape. But he had a powerful voice. There were those who said they could hear him preach a mile and a quarter away.

It so happened that Elkins wanted to visit his two sons, Hodgen and Warren, who had just moved to Indiana. This meant that stopping at Pigeon Creek would be most convenient and so he agreed to come and set a date. Abe was delighted, for Elkins was in great demand.

One who was present remembered the services. "As the appointed day approached notice was given the entire neighborhood. On a bright sabbath morning the settlers of the neighborhood gathered in. Some came in carts of the rudest construction, their wheels consisting of huge boles of forest trees and the product of ax and auger; some came on horseback, two or three upon a horse, others came in wagons drawn by oxen, and still others came on foot. Taking his stand at the foot of the grave Parson Elkins lifted his voice in prayer and sacred songs and then preached a sermon. He spoke of the precious Christian woman who had gone, with the warm praise which she had deserved, and held her up as an example of true womanhood."

We have no list of the songs that were used, but there is a strong possibility the crowd sang one of Nancy's old favorites:

> "You may bury me in the east,
> You may bury me in the west,
> And we'll rise together in the morning."

Abe and Sarah had heard Nancy sing those words as she rocked them to sleep in her splint-bottomed chair. They were certain of their truth, and this comforted them as they trudged back to the empty cabin.

In the years that followed, Abe traveled far. But he never traveled beyond the memory of his "angel mother." Her influence made a mark that nothing could erase. That mark is especially evident in a letter Abe wrote to his stepbrother, John D. Johnston, at the time of his father's illness. Dated January 12, 1851, it reads:

"I sincerely hope Father may yet recover his health, but at all events tell him to remember to call upon, and confide in, our great, and good, and merciful Maker, who will not turn away from him in any extremity. He notes the fall of a sparrow, and numbers the hairs of our heads; and He will not forget the dying man who puts his trust in Him. Say to him that if we could meet now, it is doubtful whether it would not be more painful than pleasant; but that if it is his lot to go now, he will soon have a joyous meeting with many loved ones gone before; and where the rest of us, through the help of God, hope ere to join them.

"Affectionately,
"A. Lincoln"

Nancy Hanks died at thirty-five. But the world knows she did not live in vain!

The grave of Nancy Hanks.
—Courtesy, Indiana Department of Conservation

SOURCES

In gathering material for this book, I have followed the Lincoln Trail through Kentucky, Indiana and Illinois; have made several visits to the Library of Congress; the National Archives; and called at the Lincoln Life Insurance Company in Fort Wayne, Indiana, where the largest Lincoln collection in the world is housed. In addition, I have carried on a rather wide correspondence.

Many books have been consulted. The following, however, have been especially helpful:

BARTON, WILLIAM E., *The Women Lincoln Loved*. Bobbs Merrill, 1927.

───── *The Life of Abraham Lincoln*. Educational Press by Bobbs Merrill, 1925.

BEVERIDGE, ALBERT J., *Abraham Lincoln*. Houghton Mifflin, 1928.

EARLE, ALICE MORSE, *Home Life in Colonial Days*. Macmillan, 1919.

EDGINGTON, FRANK E. *A History of the New York Avenue Presbyterian Church*. New York Avenue Presbyterian Church, 1961.

HORNER, HARLAN HOYT, *The Growth of Lincoln's Faith*. Abingdon, 1939.

JOHNSON, WILLIAM J., *Abraham Lincoln the Christian*. Abingdon, 1913.

JONES, EDGAR DEWITT, *Lincoln and the Preachers*. Harper, 1948.

LORANT, STEFAN, *The Life of Abraham Lincoln*. The New American Library, 1954.

NEWMAN, RALPH G., *Lincoln for the Ages*. Pyramid Books, 1960.

SANDBURG, CARL, *Lincoln Collector*. Harcourt Brace, 1949.

―――――*Abraham Lincoln, The Prairie Years.* Harcourt Brace, 1926.
VAN NATTER, FRANCIS MARION, *Lincoln's Boyhood.* Public Affairs Press, 1963.
WARREN, LOUIS A., *Lincoln's Youth, Indiana Years Seven to Twenty-one* 1816-1830. Appleton, Century, Crofts, 1959.